To [illegible]

All good things,

John [illegible]

Xmas 2011

Only that which bears the
imprint of our choice, our taste
and our desire can be beautiful;
our 'idée maîtresse'.

MARCEL PROUST

Galerie d'Amour

JOHN POWLS

Illustrated by

RICHARD & KAY SPARE

Published by

POETRY@MMD : READING : ENGLAND

For all the artists whose work
has provided inspiration.

Prima fuit. Finis erit.
JP 1998

Contents

Fermata

Fermata

FOR CYGNUS

My close
Panorama
Easy, morning
Sun lifts the veil
Mist from the pines
Desiring
Scenes of green
And grey.

My close
Panorama
Easy, morning
Sun lifts the veil
Dawn from your sleep
Desiring
Scenes of cream
And ivory.

Fermata.

Inhabited silence
Before artist hand
Strokes first
Mark warm colours
Out
Of the ordinary
Canvas of day
Light, ready.

Landscapes and seascapes

Fire disputes the common ground

Dusk.
Deep summer;
What passes
Between us?
The sky has changed,
Sun burning
Obscured by smoke
On the horizon
Those many desert days,
Fevered hot
Tinder, brittle, snap;
Judgement
Fuel fired
No spontaneous combustion,
Who knows where
The spark comes from;
Distorting lens,
Dry storm lightning
Discarded shard
Of something smashed,
Long smouldering ember
Of some fire before,
Not forgotten,
Some burning issue.
Driven breath,
Compelled
In the heat
Of the moment
Fans the flame
Blazing

Consuming passion
Eats the air
Pursuing scorched
Earth policy
Charred administration.

Does it die
Exhausted
Quenched, resolved
Healed by
Changing sky.

Does it leave
New life
On learning
Earth
Or choking ash
On barren waste
And fingers burned?

The soft machine

FOR SEXTUS

Poems are
Generated
Where The River
Flows through
The Soft Machine

One eternal river
One flow, knowing.
Current, concurrent
Perpetual, constant
Not unchanging,
Only perspectives
Alter
Points of view.

Deep sourced
Subtle subterranean
Spaces;
Some explored,
Many still
Unvisited
Forced through
Some intractable
Element
Awaiting understanding,
Seeding conservation
Needing conversation
With the habitable
Surface always
Ready
To be known.

Burst into view
Clear full rush
Sometimes
Tear full rush
Tearful rush
Cadence cascade
Light and shade,
Impatient.
Run the course,
Cut the mark,
Experience
Moving
Through now,
Through ages.

Liquid cathedral
Waterfalls walls
Of white noise
Into vaulted space
For a share
Of creation.

Crash, rage, foam, break;
Passion
Demands the way;
Roll, surge, caress, lick;
Dark and incandescent
Serpent and Venus
Curve continuity
Seduced

Sociable surface
Always accessible,
Gentle expansive,
Unrelenting
Hidden depths
Afford
Hidden power.

Inviting undertow
Could pull you
Under
When you are
Ready
To live.

November

Across
Open country
Full floods
Melting moon
Coined silver
In milky shallows
Of sweetwater sky.
I wonder why
I only see
Shaped art
Sleeping hills
You silhouetted
The lie of the land
When what was planned
Was the truth
Of my hand
Contouring you
Still I reach out
Missing you.

Evening clouds

Am
i
isis
cold
blue
art wide sky
vapour white
sun gifted
sunblood
warm colours
brush stroke
calligraphy
a language
ancient
simple and profound
i have time to touch
i
feel meaning
mark me
alive.

Sunday home

Dwelling dew
Single bell note
Born new
Honeysuckle breeze
Scents slow
Swaying trees
A moment
Falls open
Revealing ripe
Lazy Sunday
At the edge
Of towns
English Summer
Morning blue.

Fairground

On the surface
Face values
Common ground
Unobtrusively
Burrowed through
Tunnels
Of love.

Cedars

Late
Snow on cedars
Bends boughs
Bearing
Dreams' burden,
Almost but never
Touching
Waiting earth.
Sudden sun
Surprise
Expected warm,
Shivers relief,
Regains their
Spring;
Long weight
Is over.
I have
Seen you
Again.

Cubist lovesong: Tate Embankment

What is this day
Made
For us alone
Out
Of the ordinary
Common place
Formed built,
Occurring
Found elements
Placed
By many
Careless intended
Tribute paid
For just this
Moment.

No

No vague skies
No ordinary clouds
Messengers
Dealing
In certainty
The sincerest
Form of mockery
Properly irreverent
Read the sticks
Read the stones
In the garden
Nothing stems
Caricature curves
Course colours
No
Throwaway lines
Straight to
The point.

The passion

A clearing sky
Soft gaze
Of tender moon
Lights
On moment
Of stillness
And silence;
The plane leaves
Relaxing cling,
Their dear drops
The passion
Summer storm
Spent;
In that time
All the beauty
Of the world.

Pietra, sempre pietra: the Touchstone

Granite land
Marks
A dream
Of rivers
Brightly threading
Trees and grasses
Open moor
Free stone feel
The space
Place is fate
Sense and self
Choice and craving
Unstill life
Movement
The changing
Landscape
Where nothing
Separates us
From the earth
And all times
Are now
Also then
And ever
We will
Loving
Touchstone
Face forward
In order to know
Where we must be
What we must do
In order to grow.

Place Vendôme

Trompe l'oeil
Loose
Faux mausoleum
Cold scaffold
Partly covers
As yet not
Re-born
Poles apart
Half melted
From the building
Passion
Blue roofs
Moonsliced
Pitched shining
Windows
Yellow white
Long lidded
Lying sleep
Sound
Steel looks
Wet wrapped
Warm mist
Drag draped
Devoré
Across evening
Not round
Pounding hearts
We began
To exchange
Faces
Veiled kiss.

Florence

Where we are
Where others
Have been
Still traces
The universe
Has no secrets
Innocent of guile
Naive
For discovery
Mapped by ideas
Lines meet
Through here
There is more
Than is simply
Present
Though what is
Is wonder
Full on
Touching terms
The people
Every age
Take a grip
Adopting shape
The timeless
Propertius Milton
Galileo Rossini
Michaelangelo
Walk together
With us

Through piazzi
Via towards
Slow Arno
Constant
What objects
Do we make
That hold
Yester
Day to day
And to
Morrow.

Shore

Shore
Lines, signs
Of storms when
Tense, forced
The horizon apart,
Rent
For the elemental
Savage tenancy.

Cathedral of dark light

Where the light
Falls

Edge of blue

Heaven
Stormdark light
Coal jet bright
Revealing
Its diamond brother

So much light
Drawn in
Beginning
To radiate rainbows
Resolved
A solid shaft
Slicing

Air to earth
Lightning fast
Caught
In stained glass
Seas silk slow.

The sea door

The water has
A long memory
Things it learned
From the air
Create movement
In return
Gentle vortex
Drawing down
Warm moon
Unlocks
Dark doors
To dawn
Where the
Naive colours
Wake into knowing
The sea door.

Shorelines

Beach
Combing
Shorelines of
A used sea
A box
Of moonlight
Overturned
Spills out
Toward me
It does not feel
The weight of water
The wait of water
Released
Flotsam bleached
Beached by
Fortune's
Bleak tides
Twist the strand
Stained with sand
Expose just
So many
Fossil records
Of your beauty
And there still
The house
On the hill
Bitter bloodshot
Careworn Camelot
Tears tears
Beneath roof
Slate blue

Moon squared
Window, paned
Stares
Out to sea
With no memory
Searching the wry
Corners of sky
Cenotaph to love
Once
Upon a time.

Blue

Behind a blue
Unsilvered mirror
Small rainbows sleep
And sunset shells
Silent light strands
Sounds of sea
Stroking shore.

Once more without feeling

Above sea rage
The scoured sky,
Great slabs of grey
Winter,
Cubist reduced
At last
One type of emptiness
Mounts another,
Unloving.
Driven by a cold
And distant body,
Shapeless and patterned
Successions of water
Prepare their coming
Foaming breaking
Sequences.
Salted, crashing
Climaxes
Run into
The sand.

Portraits

Cubism

Synthesis: Upright figure of a woman. Classical background with two towers defined by their secrets.

Wedges of mirror		
Papier mache		
Style magazines		
Some		
In French	Studied	
	Created texts	
Red red		
Printed		
Smudged tissue		
Crumpled		
Lipstick mouthed	Discrete	
	Designer labelled	
	Fashioned	
Black and white		
Photograph		
Parents turned		
Face down	Cards	Heart
At the heart	From friends	Cut
		From
		A secret
	Collage of lists	Valentine
	Mostly	Fixed to
Loose paper	Background	The sleeve
Worked	Some unseen	
Prominent		
		Three keys
		Black waxed
Sheer stroked		Leather
Strong		
A Wolford	Silk pursed	
Advert		
Smoothed		Inscribed
		Gold
		Watch
	Manolo	
	Blahnik	
	Patently	
Litter unused	Scattered used	Train tickets

Cubism

ANALYSIS: RECLINING
FIGURE OF A WOMAN

Played out;
Awaiting play
The truth
Of the hand
Defining lines
Marked contrasts
Lavish and complex
Planes
Material geometry
Cream to ivory
Body of evidence
For the passion
Savage soul
Polished and black
Against
The grain
Reflex
Angles wired
Pitched
High action
Across the bridge
Contemplations
Of the circle
Conjugated
Shape between
Looked at slowly
Measured

By desire unbound
Form of
Soft, distant
Tower rises
Relieved
Of its field
Prominent.

Earthchild

The child
That never was,
Wanted but denied
By will,
Loved and mourned.
A study in becoming,
Never realised

Born of the deep
Architecture
Of the ancient earth;
Hand hewn and cut
Landscapes
Of works
Create space

In which
We place
Landscapes
Of intent,
Bare and complicated
The body unyielding
By choice
Whispers
'I am soft inside'.

The child
That never was,
Ageless, silent
All these years
For, by nature
Fact, once uttered
Is unstable;

The unwritten
Law of Love
The unknown
Principle discovered,
That the right one
Arrives too soon...
...or too late

Yet you are born
of the true marriage
Of two minds, two bodies,
Two souls, two hearts.
You are seen
In our eyes
You are loved;
Sharp consolation.

Heroic child,
Distributed being,
Trailing narrative
Clouds from the peak
Gathered in
Stories
Word of mouth
Promised
To honour and duty
The shaper
Of legends
To come.
Present through
Your absence.

Often the rolling sky
Grieves,
Lacking the gift
Of anguish,
Throws on
Your unused shroud
And weeps;
Dry tears,
The mind's eye
Memorial
To time immemorial
Polished
By love's touch
Care worn

Until you are
Delivered.
Our child
That never was

Mosaique en soi grege

Making
A picture
Mosaic
Little pieces
Of irridescent
Behaviour from
A warm heart
Of raging hues
No
Little peaces
Catch
The light
A single image
Starts
From the surface
Raw silken
Beauty
I see you
In everything
This way.

Long train running

There's a long
Train running
Processing
With hiss
And rasp
Someone breathing
Confidences
Through the night
That fell
So heavy
So massive
That nothing
Escapes
Even light
Has flown
To see dawn
Dufy drawn
Down voices
Soft stilled
The view from
The window
Is your own
Quiet reflection
Recalling...
Me?
Or are you only
In love
with secrets.

A Matisse likeness

FOR ALISON

In that moment
I watched your eyes
Becoming
The colour of lost love.

Watched you
As we noised silently
Anthologising
Those moments kept
Secret scraps sorting
Mind mined turned
Familiar wound words
For meaning strung out
Roped by regret
Knotted by longing;
Those ties that you know
No longer bind
Re-asserted realised
released
Possessed
and possessing
Self starting
The kick inside
In that moment
We were joined
In art.
Line of desire
Desire of line

Opening ourselves

Not contingent
A need
Understood
In that instrument
There is not the
Precision

Colour is the
closest to feeling
Least rational
The control
of a language
before
Language

You are describing
What I have known.

Opening ourselves

Proud

Where is she going
Mother?
Asked her father,
As the queen
In the eighth year
Of her reign
Left the room
Again
As though forever,
Definite always.
Gentle, her mother
Placed the comfort,
Her reminding hand
On his empty,
Gestured arm
They both knew
The unspoken answer
That she was
Already
The woman
She was
To become.

Wash

Brought to
My senses
Water colours
On a wash
Of tenderness
For you.

Inner light

Suddenly you
With your
Simple grace
Of perfect art
Inner light
Sure spirit of
A truant summer
Fragrant
Definite,
I am warmed
Through again.

Missing

Are you
Becoming
A portrait
Of gaps
And shadows,
What of substance
Deepening gulf
Spreading bars
Beats, ticked off
Are you
Missing
Me too...

Drowning

We never say
So much
As when we
Don't know
Quite what
To say
Empty rhetoric
From
Dull reservoirs
Drown my words.

Element 5

Often
I have
Metaphored you
As an element
Most often
Water
Realised
This is less
Than you are
An element
In your own
Right

Discovered
This is why
I am
Truly
In my
Element

At last.

Intense

Starting
Out I looked
Intently
At your lips
Your eyes
You spoke
With listening.
When I replied
I invested
Every word
With meaning
Hoping for
Interest
Feeling
Still
I'm paying

Attention
To what
Matters.

Capturing

Capturing
This moment
Freeing ourselves
In its entirety
In its eternity
No time
Better
Than now
Transcribing
The adventures
Of the senses
In this close
Still
Together
I offer you
My pulse
I give you
My breath
I am alive
With yours.

Middle 8 from an imaginary jazz standard

You are the poem
That scans like
A river.

You are the poem
That rhymes like
A sky.

You are the poem
With rhythms of
An ocean.

You are the poem
Where my voice
Learned to fly.

And how it yearned
To fly.

Funfair

In the hall
Of mirrors
We laugh
Being
Implausibly happy
That everything
We do
Is outside in
And downside up.
Here you go
Creeping
Up on me
When I most
Expect it.
Catching me
Awares.
Come up on
My sighted side
You constant
Surprise
Reflecting invention.

Autoportraits

The faction

What you are about
to read is true;
only the names
have been changed
to protect
the rhythm
of the poems.

Learning

Gone silent
Midnight
Storm of wills
Clears contradiction
In terms
Small hours
Restless
Digging towards
The buried sun.
Bruised
Purple petulance
Dark to day
Reality dawns last
Star fades away
Pinpoints:
I write
No epics
For I
Am no
Hero.

Moore

The gestures of your sleep
the naked shapes of your clothed
body revealing
stone   wood   water
I remark; I thought to see
all form is sensuality
I am simply busy with words
burn with a harder flame
the invented me is the truest now
from any angle;
from a conventional standpoint
my heart is in the wrong place
surfaces admire it without wanting
stare too long into the icy sunlight
and see reflections.

Painting in the mirror

I am looking
Hard
Glass eyed
Will not
Want not
See darkly
With my mind's
Only eye
The image
Of me
Drawing in
Always holding
Its distance.
Shallow they
Who judge not
By appearances
Mystery in
The apparent
Experienced
Not imagined
I render
The possible
Reading who
Has authorship
Of this
Appearance
On further
Reflection;

I have not
Always
Liked what
I see
But
I know
It is art.

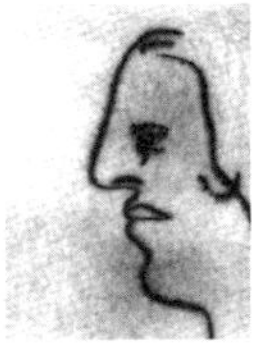

Prayers for the secular

Rarely frank
I find
Soliloquy
No assurance
No insurance
No third party
No good
Talking to
So more needed
Earnest rhetoric
With only me
To convince
On this cold
Cold night
With its
New leaves
Small black beads
Cold sweat
Broken
Out of branches
Its unsafe
Sky taste
Of salt stars
Crystal
On tongue tip
Its hand
Mirror moon
Hoared
My muslin breath

Ribboning
Thin silent
Whistle
In the dark;

Can't
Cant
Catch
Me.

Restoration

Once
I put
My feelings
Inside a box
Under pressure
Applied
Crystallised
Rather than be
Crushed
Faults found
Shattered shards
Shrapnel out
Indiscriminate
Casualties.

Situations

FOR HOWARD

How did I
Come
To this
Dark place
Lose
The touch

A lover

Miniature betrayals
Of feelings
Small red and blue
Situations.

Challenge

How long
Have you seen
Through me
Since I was
Unedited
A first draft
An intense
Sweet passage
In a longer
Piece
Or now
Written off
Completely
What is your view?

Tokens

I have kept
The sticks and stones
That you used
To break my bones
But it was
Your words
That hurt me,
What you said
Torn too
Shred
Crying?
Shame.

Song

I don't always
Sing
From happiness
To anger
Ranging raging
To moment
Of content

Constant

I am
Contrast marked
Fleeting reassurance
Nature and recreation
Seaspray rainbow
Curious
I have no time
For harsh fantasy
I need
Romance
Reality made
Since we are
Specially recognised
Portrait of
More shapely chaos
You could
Always
Regard me
A challenge
Constant
As fashion
I shall
Only want
You
Yester
Day to day
And to
Morrow.

Lost and found out

All my life
I seem
To be
Trying
To avoid
Being found
Out
Climbing
Reaching
Beyond here
Lies
Footholds
Hand over hand
Anticipating
The fall from
That smooth
Hollow hearted
Shining sphere
Spinning slowly
In the way
Of the fear
But not falling
Saving
From my own
Grace;

You have
Found me
Out
Looked at me
Unblinking
And yet
You love me
Still
Not moving
Always moving
Everyday miracle.

Nudes

Drawing from life

With eyes
Half closed
Realising
Voluptuous approach
Of new perspective
Owned by closeness
Seductive steals
Over me;
I sense you
Taste by taste
By tongue tip
Hot infusion
Scents ribboned
Round form
Understanding space
Enfolds creating
Instrument
And shapes it
Lasting
The truth
Of my hand
Contours you
All beauty
At hand
I trace its line
Original
With my defining
Fingers
To know.

I begin
To draw
On experience.

Sleeping

I picture us
Navigating night
On a new sea
Of hours
Sound
Star cushioned
Together sleeping
We have made
Talking pictures
For a tender
And ruthless eye
Touching verse
In motion
Framed
Embracing fierceness
Locked limbs
Disorderly mix
Of ingredients
Making sense
Exclamation marked
At last long
Curled
Against your back
Fashioned comma
Serving purpose
Paused
Against your
Languid elegant
Phrase.

Bathing in light

FOR PIERRE AND MARTHE

Just
After heartrise
We annoint
With perfumed
Light
Recreation
Brings us
Limb live
Again private
Ritual mutual
Invention
Faith affirming
Constant
Art functions
To explore
Familiar traces
Warm geography
Feel touch
Colours body
Fingers caress
Living ground
Straight
See soft swell
Morning
Respond languid
Light to look
Intimating
Seductive awakening
Anew.

Naked

For you
I am dangerous
Naked
Wild and alive
Under
Presentable clothes
All day
Stand ready
The red cry
Hard and fast
Beginning
To melt
For your
Heat.

Still life

A smaller splash

Floating in
A small square
Reflecting
Lap slapping hypnotically
Intimate as a dream
Mediterranean blue pool
Gauche mosaic gamely tries
Representing
Mediterranean surroundings
Like the efforts
Of the inept schoolboy
I really am
Considering
Thinking of
Not thinking of
You
I am lying
In wait
For the next poem
It is in
No hurry.

Divine chorus

Standing in
The red room
Drinking colour
Through my eyes

As the wood
Turned to water
Blue outside
The window

See real sea
On paper
Watercolour
And gouache

As the wood
Turned to water
Blue outside
The window

Inside and
Outside seeing
Through another
View clearly

As the wood
Turned to water
Blue outside
The window.

Nameless

FOR JEANETTE

What
In creation
Move in solid
Flesh rock
Mineral metal
Like fish in water
Birds in air
What is their motion
That is not walking
Flying swimming
Not burrowing nor art
What physics
What functions
Mandate form
What proportions
Filamental strung
Out massed
Compacted
A hot dark
Matter
What biochemistry
Sustains breeds
Life cycling;
Nameless.

Can they
Penetrate
The polished
Rubbing pointed
Stone heart
Of my heart
Leave no
Trace
Tell me
My secret.
Like you did.

Fretwork

Piecing
Together
Satisfying shapes
Jigsawn
Their colours
Their feel
Divert and
Engage as
They build
Towards their
Solution
Fitting in
A world
Within reach.

Sometimes
When a picture
Is made
By the gaps
Still formed
Fretworked
Insight
I slip through
To my
Child view

As far
As I can
See
Close at hand
Happily.

Roses in the snow

Singular odyssey
Time between times
Expression
Becoming
A dead tongue;
Cold scrolling,
Unused, unspoken,
Unread, unknowing;
Laying roses
In the snow;
Empty beauty,
Frozen futile.

There
Is
Still life
Arrested essence;
Distilled,
Living stream
When even
My own noise
Stills;
Moment;
And you
Hold me
Still.
There is
Still life.

Meadows in Spring

White air
Wrapped
In sun
Soul of winds
Soft hurricanes
Hosts breeze
Blizzard of colours
Dance each leaf
And stems sway
And a heart
Reflected
In the earth;
Over a sky
Of wild meadow
Flowers
I walk
Each so beautiful
They could be
A thought of you
Fresh as today's
Last kiss
Lingering
On my lips.

The Croft

Essence
Wisteria heavy
Hanging
On the evening air.
The ribbon of its
Unravelling
Caught me
Unawares
All the power
Of our history
Romance
Almost inscrutable
Lying innocent
Tempting
Over the welcome
Trap of memory.
I was lured
And fell
Headlong
Back to the scene.

Leaving

Sensing regret
As I scan
Our room
What powerful
Alluring strategies
Things that know
Us
Can invent
Animate inanimate
When they guess
My leaving
In welcome
Warm conspiracy
They seek
To detain me
Willing capture
The flowers
And the card
Left for you
On our table
Look as though
Placed
By twilight purpose
On the surface of a lake.

Azul y Blanco

Each day
For our story
A new page
Broad and sky
Blue
Vapour white
To write
Turn to
Burn to
Red and yellow
Move to memory;
Watch with me
This blue
Is the colour
Of my dreams.

Invited to
Sweet exaggerated
Days of interest
And desires
Big armfuls
Of warm light
Stay together
Hearts unlocked
Learn the colours
Go light
Understanding
Circles round us.

Autumn's voice

Now, the days
Grown shorter
I hear
The onset
Of Winter
In your voice
I struggle
To hear
Indian Summer.

Fate

Born
Of yearning,
Every poem
Needs
Some unrequited
Love;
Every love
Needs
Some unrequited
Poem.
It is our
Fate.

Solitaire

Then
A single
Tear
Bitter souvenir
Sharp and bright
Solitaire
Adorned your eye
I
Never gave you
Jewels before.

How could I
When that
Is where
I
Learned to fly
Easily
Sadly.

The muse

It is as if
Like me
My art
Creation
Can't take
Its eyes
Off you
Watching
Wanting
Drenched by
Your own sun
Elegant presence
A light
Filled space
Thinking
Fore and back
And ground
Flux fixed
Stillness
Disturbing
What I am
We are
Making me.

The bliss before

FOR AUGUSTE

Remember this
The naked
Kiss

Relaxes
The mind
Concentrates
The body
Unhooked
Engaged

Remember this
The naked kiss.

Dream

Night
On a new sea
A whole raft
Of lemons
Yellow
Half-moon high
Holds
A ribbon
Rippling light
From horizon
To trailing hands
Twined, turn
My face to
The cinnamon
Breeze
Breathe
You in.

Retreat

Wind with
The first whiff
Of winter
Stirs the dry
Stalks rustling
Rumours round
Though we talk
Of future campaigns
And victory
We have struck
Our standard and
This feels
Like retreat
If not
Defeat.

Sunburn

Looking forward,
One day this summer
Will end, hot
As we now are,
Right in the sun
Blindingly bright.
As the thought
Comes
Relief is there
In the shape
Of your cool
Fingertips, already?
Soon enough
For our sun
In its abbreviated
Form
To become again
Everyone's sun
Smiling down;
This sort of sadness
Is best expressed
By a smile.

The still life of flowers

Sunflower

You
Sweet deranged
Outrageous
Flowering of sun
Spun threads
Drawn from life
Giving light
Golden warm
Bright shade
Of a feeling
Growing to be
Framed
The image
The one
And now only
Ambitioned
Sunflowers
Heart's desire.

Lilies

Restless
Digging towards
The buried sun
Bruised
Burning daylight
Purple yellow
Petulance peeling
Layers
Clear contradictions
In terms
Surface smiles.

Poppies

On the field
Of morning
Misted
Watermarked
In parchment
Reddening spread
Of a blush
Poppies
Indiscrete kiss
Promise
Of passion.

Iris

Night fired
Rainbow
Blue pearl
Lustred
Iris
Relaxed alert
Reflecting on
Sharp sheer
Soft enamelled
Faberge
Leaves
Pointed out.

Exotica

FOR LORCA

Except me
No one understood
The perfume, ever
The blush magnolia
Of your belly;
No one heard
The low moan, ever
Of leaves lush
And lascivious
Pierced by stem
Of desire;
No one touched
Fleshed flowers, ever
The creamy camellia
Swell or orchids
Waxy red throat;
No one tasted
The nectar, ever
Honeyed and salted
Delicious primeval
And the fruit
Of wild figs;
Except me.

I want you green, ever
Ever, ever my ecstasy's garden.

Petals

That summer
Day
Treacle time
Measured
By beats,
A different clock
Sweet attention
Not paying
Forgetting
Staying
Here and now
Then
From the garden
Evening pale
Yellow
Briar roses
In your hair
Weep
Their petals
To your
Not yet cold
Shoulder.
Where to
From here?

Miniatures

Formed

Formed
Opening
You are
Rose-wet
Wild and delicate
By our love
Making.

Fingering

Shadow words
By my hand
Finger honey
Peach drool
Luscious produce
Sweet friend
Whisper Goddess
Shadow words
By my hand.

Away

You, there I
Yearn
Like a ship
Tethered
To the quay
Of a sort
Of choice.

Disguise

Dreams
Dress sleep
Shadow Clothing
In disguise
Coutured
Savage things
Whispering
Take my hand.

Partner

Lasted
Resolved
I came
For giving
Now I'm there
For the
Taking.

Geordie's kids

Fertile, forming
Rich brown
Warm mash
Stirring
Fuelling, escape
Ensuring
Captivation.

Memory lain?

Now
He's a memory
Lain
Sudden pain
Wane and drain
Like an endless
Day of rain...
But here he comes
Again.

Geometry

Seeking form
And relationship
He draws
Triangles
And not
Circles
And doing so
He draws them
Closer and closer
Apart.

Ikon

Ikon

The
Varnished truth.

Sounding ikon
Unwritten saying
Air strung
With promises
Lift the veil
Mystery
In case
We can see
Through it
Romance
And emptiness
Of pure style
Codes of
Hand and eye
Co-ordination
Studied and
Precise echoes
In the body
Miss
Gilded myth.

Glowing
Gold and black
A surface
Looking back
An interior
Black and gold
Colour me cold
Revelation.

Cruel colours
Staying sleep
No rest
To test
Tollhouses
All doors open
Pass through
To the troubled
Roads choices
For the undevout
Unbelievable.

Abstracts

I

WRITE

AS A

SCULPTURE

WOOD

SOUND

CONCRETE

Look!

LOOK
AT ME

I
AM TRYING
NOT TO
SQUANDER
YOUR GAZE

Sounding out a Mondrian composition

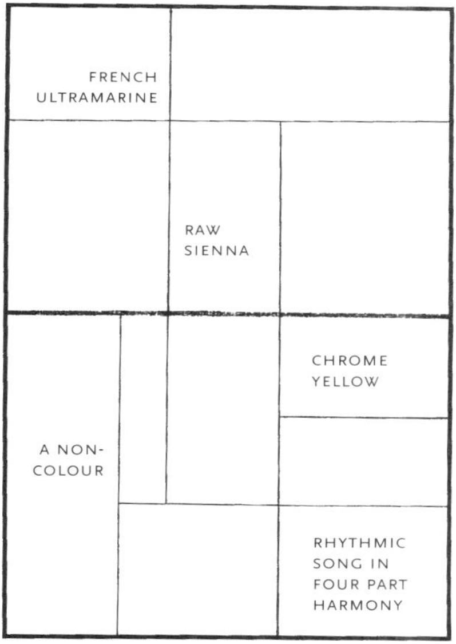

A LONG FORGOTTEN SUBLIME CURVE

line of desire **desire of line**

Frames

Frames

We paint
Our life
Inside different
Frames
We select
Reference
Colours
Plain ornate
Seen unseen;
Here
Is one

Late night
Bricolage
And quarrels
Muffled
Bass beats
Tuneless
Footsteps fall
Door full
Stop
Listeners
Car horns
Drift on
A careless air
Layered
Through French
Windows
Church clock chimes
Quartering hours

Ripe time
Fruits of
Varying size
And colour
The dripping
Of watered pots
From balcony
To yard
A shard
Of the often
Unconsidered.

Do we
Complete the picture
Change them
Or the other
Way.

JOHN POWLS *has written poetry for over 25 years. He has been published extensively in poetry journals, anthologies and newspapers in recent years. He has broadcast his work on radio and television and is a regular performer at major festivals and other poetry venues. His first collection 'Dartmoor Dreams', a collaboration with photographer Carol Ballenger, was published by Devon Books in 1995. This work was subsequently developed into a longer libretto for a five movement lyric piece for string quartet by composer Alan Danson. This was recorded by the Rowan Quartet and John Powls and released on cassette, also in 1995.*

Further examples of John Powls' work and those of close collaborators in the 'Arts Live' partnership can be seen at their website: members.aol.com/artslive1/.
This includes details of multimedia projects which have attracted support from the Arts Council via National Lottery grants.

John is currently working on collaborative projects with artists Richard Spare and Lindsay Mullen and a millennium project to raise a new menhir stone, 'The Touchstone' on Dartmoor, the first for several thousand years, which will be inscribed with one of his poems.